How Artists See

Animals

Karen Hosack

www.heinemann.co.uk/library

To order:
☎ Phone 44 (0) 1865 888066
🖹 Send a fax to 44 (0) 1865 314091
💻 Visit the Heinemann Bookshop at www.heinemann.co.uk/library to browse our catalogue and order online.

First published in Great Britain by Heinemann Library, Halley Court, Jordan Hill, Oxford OX2 8EJ, part of Harcourt Education.
Heinemann is a registered trademark of Harcourt Education Ltd.

Editorial: Andrew Farrow and Dan Nunn
Design: Ron Kamen and Celia Floyd
Illustrations: Jo Brooker
Picture Research: Mica Brancic and Charlotte Lippman
Production: Viv Hichens

Originated by Dot Gradations Ltd
Printed and bound in Hong Kong and China by South China Printing Company

The paper used to print this book comes from sustainable resources.

ISBN 0 431 93217 4
08 07 06 05 04
10 9 8 7 6 5 4 3 2 1

British Library Cataloguing in Publication Data

Hosack, Karen
 Animals. – (How artists see)
 1. Animals in art – Juvenile literature
 2. Art appreciation – Juvenile literature
 I. Title
 704.9'432

A full catalogue record for this book is available from the British Library.

Acknowledgements
The publishers would like to thank the following for permission to reproduce photographs:

© ADAGP, Paris and DACS, London 2004 p. **10** (Bridgeman Art Library); Archives Charmet p. **26** (Bridgeman Art Library); © ARS, NY and DACS, London 2004 p. **9** (Bridgeman Art Library); Burrell Collection, Glasgow, Scotland, © Glasgow City Council (Museums) p. **20** (Bridgeman Art Library); Damien Hirst p. **5** (courtesy of Jay Jopling/White Cube); David Kemp p. **22**; © Frederick Warne & Co., 1902, 2002 p. **19 right**; Index p. **7** (Bridgeman Art Library); Graphische Sammlung Albertina, Vienna pp. **12** (Bridgeman Art Library), **18** (Bridgeman Art Library); © Interfoto p. **17** (Bridgeman Art Library); © Landmann Patrick p. **25** (Corbis Sygma); © Leeds Museums and Art Galleries, Temple Newsam House p. **24** (Bridgeman Art Library); National Gallery, London pp. **16** (Bridgeman Art Library), **21 top** (Bridgeman Art Library); National Gallery Picture Library pp. **4, 27**; Peter Willi p. **21 bottom** (Bridgeman Art Library); Rebecca Hossack Gallery, London p. **13**; Royal Pavilion, Libraries and Musuems, Brighton and Hove p. **23 right**; Sonnabend Gallery, New York p. **19 left**; Tate London 2004 pp. **6, 8 bottom, 14, 23 left, 28** (© Salvador Dali, Gala-Salvador Dali Foundation, DACS, London 2004); Tudor Photography pp. **11 x 3, 15 x 3, 29 x 3**.

Cover photograph (*Van Gogh's Cat* by Fred Aris, 1991) reproduced with permission of Bridgeman Art Library/© DACS 2004, courtesy of Portal Gallery, London.

Every effort has been made to contact copyright holders of any material reproduced in this book. Any omissions will be rectified in subsequent printings if notice is given to the Publishers.

Contents

Words printed in bold letters, **like these**,
are explained in the Glossary.

How artists see animals

Throughout history, artists around the world have used animals as subjects in their work. Many artists and designers enjoy exploring the beautiful patterns, scaly skins and furry coats of animals.

Kitchen Scene with Christ in the House of Martha and Mary by Diego Velázquez, around 1618

The two women in this painting are preparing fish for supper. The artist has painted shiny scales on the fish, and the eyes are bright and glassy. The fish look very real.

The Physical Impossibility of Death in the Mind of Someone Living by Damien Hirst, 1991

LIMERICK COUNTY LIBRARY

This **sculpture** is made from a real tiger shark in a glass tank. The tank is filled with a liquid called formaldehyde, which stops the shark from rotting. Even though the shark is definitely dead, it looks as if it could break out of its tank at any moment. Scary!

Using lines

The simplest drawings use just lines. Here, Henri Gaudier-Brzeska has drawn a dog using thick bold lines. See how the artist has used only a few long strokes. This is more difficult than it looks. Try it!

A Dog by Henri Gaudier-Brzeska, around 1913

Try this!

Have a go at drawing something using only a few long lines. The trick is always to look at what you are drawing, not the paper.

Cave painting by prehistoric people, painted more than 10,000 years ago

Thousands of years ago **prehistoric** people made line drawings on cave walls using **flint**, chalk and burnt sticks. The drawings were sometimes filled in with paints they made from clay, **minerals** and metals. The prehistoric people probably made these pictures to bring them good luck when they were hunting.

Using simple shapes

Can you tell what animal this shape is? What country do you think the sign came from? The sign was designed to be seen clearly at a glance. It warns drivers of possible danger from animals in the road.

The artist below has used some simple shapes for his picture 'Two Cows'. Do they look like cows to you?

Two Cows by Peter Kinley, 1983–85

In this sculpture the artist has focused on a spider's legs. Spiders have lots of legs. Because they are usually quite small the artist has looked at the overall shape of a spider. These shapes have been hung in a **mobile**. When the mobile moves in the wind it looks like a spider crawling along.

Silhouettes

A **silhouette** is a dark shape on a light background. Pierre Bonnard used silhouettes to make this playful picture of two dogs. If you look carefully you can see one dog is lying on its back with its legs in the air. The other dog is about to leap. The artist has **textured** the background to look like grass.

Two Dogs Playing
by Pierre Bonnard,
1891

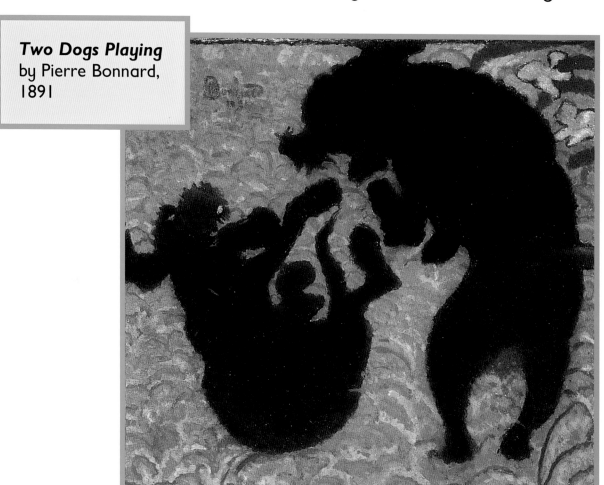

Make your own silhouette picture

You will need:

- *two pieces of paper (one dark and one light)*
- *a pencil*
- *scissors*
- *glue*
- *paints or coloured pencils.*

Instructions:

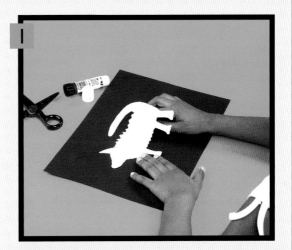

1 Draw the outline of an animal and cut it out. You could draw a pet that is sitting in front of you or copy a picture from a magazine, photograph or book. When you have finished, glue the drawing on to the dark piece of paper.

2 Cut around the animal shape. This will be your silhouette. Then draw a design on the light piece of paper with paints or coloured pencils. Remember to use only light colours because this will be the background.

3 Glue your silhouette animal shape dark side up on to the background paper. Your dark paper silhouette should now be on top of your background!

Line used for texture

Rembrandt sketched this elephant using a sharp pencil. Look at the small feathery lines he has used to show the elephant's skin. They make it look wrinkled and rough. It is easier to control a pencil when drawing small sketchy lines.

An Elephant by Rembrandt van Rijn, around 1637

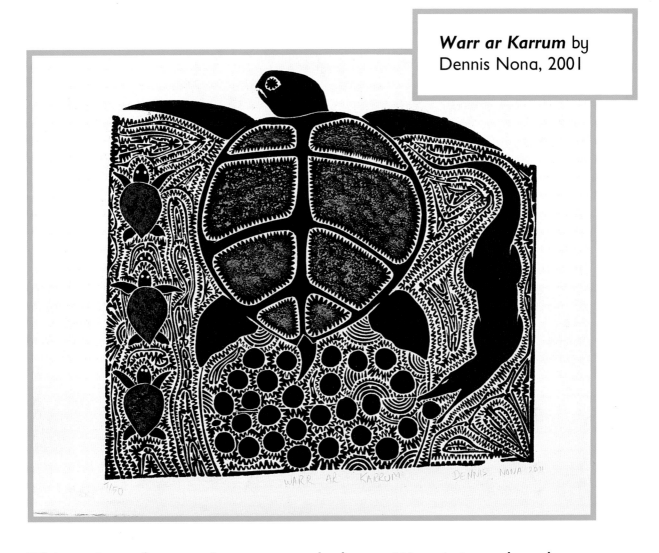

Warr ar Karrum by Dennis Nona, 2001

This print of a turtle was made by cutting into a hard cork material called **lino**. To cut it an artist uses special tools. The tools make lines and dig out **textures**. When the design is finished, ink is rolled over the lino. It is then turned over and printed on to paper or **fabric**. All the areas that are cut away in the lino design will not print.

13

Printing designs

This is an example of a **lithograph**. The artist draws a design on **limestone** or a metal plate with greasy ink or a wax crayon. Printing ink is then rolled over the surface. The ink sticks to the grease or wax. Then a piece of paper is smoothed over the stone or metal. This produces the final print.

Jelly Fish by Prunella Clough, 1950

Make your own simple print

You will need:

- *a shiny surface, e.g. a piece of plastic or a tray*
- *poster paint*
- *a piece of paper.*

Instructions:

1. Spread a layer of poster paint over a shiny surface. This will be your printing plate. (Important! Make sure you have permission to use this surface first.) Next, draw a design into the paint. You should use something pointed for this, like a pencil or a knitting needle. You could also try making patterns with other objects, such as your fingers. Make sure you have a paper towel handy though!

2. Very gently place a piece of paper over the paint. When you have done this, pull back the paper slowly, to reveal your design. You will need to do this before the paint dries, so be quick!

3. You should now have your finished print.

Tiger stripes

Henri Rousseau probably never saw a real tiger in a jungle in his life! This picture is from his imagination. Rousseau has painted stripes on the tiger. These patterns help the tiger hide in the long grass. We call this camouflage.

Tiger in a Tropical Storm (Surprised!) by Henri Rousseau, 1891

Tiger by Franz Marc, 1912

Franz Marc used bright and unusual colours in this painting. He painted jagged shapes for the jungle leaves. The striped pattern on the tiger's coat merges with the leaves. The tiger looks dangerous as it sits very still. It is waiting to pounce on its prey.

17

Fluffy bunnies!

Dürer probably drew this hare as it sat in front of him. The hare might have run away at any time. So Dürer would have sketched the overall shape of the hare very quickly. Later, back in the studio, he would have added in its features and fluffy fur.

A Young Hare by Albrecht Dürer, 1502

Rabbit by Jeff Koons, 1986

Peter Rabbit

Beatrix Potter drew Peter Rabbit, a character in her stories. She made Peter look a little bit like a person by dressing him in a jacket.

Jeff Koons' rabbit doesn't look very fluffy at all. It is made from shiny **stainless steel**. Can you see the creases in its ears? The steel has been **moulded** to look like a child's balloon. The **sculpture** seems light enough to float away. It is actually very heavy.

Showing movement

Edgar Degas painted these racehorses and jockeys in a shower of rain. The whole painting looks blurry. Degas wanted to create a feeling of movement. He used thick brushstrokes to show the basic shapes of the horses and their riders. He also used very little detail. Degas was an **Impressionist**. This group of artists liked to paint very quickly to catch a moment in time.

Jockeys in the Rain by Edgar Degas, around 1880

Whistlejacket by George Stubbs, 1762

This is a life-size **portrait** of a racehorse called Whistlejacket. The horse is **rearing** on its **hind legs**. This makes it look wild and powerful. George Stubbs decided not to paint a background for this portrait. This makes Whislejacket the centre of attention. It also makes him look a bit like a **statue**.

Did you know?

Statues like this can be seen in many public spaces such as parks or city centres. This statue is cast in **bronze**, so it will probably last a very long time. The position of the horse's legs make it look like it is moving.

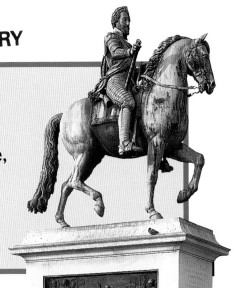

Different materials

Artists use many different materials. These dogs are made from old wellington boots. Their legs are made from whole boots. Their tails are made from the feet of boots, and their mouths are made from two toecaps!

Hounds of Geevor by David Kemp, 1998

The **ceramic** cat on the right is wearing a flowery jacket and medallion. Its cheerful face and bright colours would decorate any room nicely. Emile Gallé designed lots of these cats. He travelled to many countries looking for ideas for patterns.

The Gallé Cat
by Emile Gallé, 1880

The painting on the left uses the more traditional materials of oil paints on canvas. The girl in the picture is feeling a bit glum. Luckily she has her best friend to cheer her up!

Sympathy by Briton Rivière, 1878

23

Animals as decoration

This Japanese silk print uses butterflies and birds in its design. Their natural surroundings have inspired the other patterns in the design. The **fabric** will probably be used to make traditional Japanese clothes, such as **kimonos**.

Did you know?

Some animals have patterns on their coats so they can blend in to their surroundings. Many fashion designers, such as Christian Lacroix, have used animal patterns on the clothes they design.

Grasshopper Vase by René Lalique, 1913

René Lalique was famous for designing jewellery and glassware. He was very fond of using animals to decorate his designs. He was especially keen on insects.

Weird and strange

This **etching** by Francisco de Goya shows a nightmare. Bats and owls flap around a sleeping man's head. To protect himself he covers his head with his arms. He probably hopes he will wake up soon!

The Sleep of Reason Produces Monsters by Francisco de Goya, 1797

This scene takes place at a carnival in a city called Venice, in Italy. The people looking at the rhinoceros have almost certainly never seen one before. They probably think it looks very strange!

How very odd!

Salvador Dali liked to put unusual objects together in his **sculptures**. Here he brings together a telephone and a lobster. If the telephone rang you would have to pick it up and talk in to the tail of the lobster. How very odd! Dali belonged to a group of artists known as the **Surrealists**.

Did you know?

'Sur' at the start of a word means 'over'. So the name Surrealist means 'over real', like a fantasy or a dream.

Lobster Telephone by Salvador Dali, 1936

Make you own Surrealist animal collage

You will need:
- *old magazines*
- *glue*
- *scissors*
- *paper.*

Instructions:

1 Cut out pictures of animals and objects from magazines.

2 Try matching up different pictures of animals with different pictures of objects, using as many combinations as you like.

3 When you are happy with your combinations, glue them on the paper.

Glossary

bronze hard shiny metal made from copper and tin

ceramic something made of china, pottery or earthenware

etching design scratched on to a metal plate, which is then dipped in acid. The acid eats into the lines on the plate, which can then be used to print lots of copies.

fabric cloth made by weaving, knitting or felting fibres together

flint type of hard, grey rock

hind legs back legs

Impressionists artists who showed the effect of light and movement in their pictures

kimono a long robe with wide sleeves, worn in Japan

limestone type of rock

lino hard cork material. 'Lino' is short for 'linoleum'.

lithograph type of print made by drawing on a flat stone or metal surface with wax. When ink is added, it sticks to the wax. The stone or metal can then be used to print lots of copies.

mineral natural substance found in the Earth's surface

mobile piece of art that hangs and is able to move

mould to make something into a particular shape

portrait painting or photograph of a real person or animal

prehistoric many years ago, before records of events begin

rearing when a horse stands up on its hind legs

sculpture piece of art made from a solid material

silhouette a dark shape against a light background

stainless steel type of metal that does not rust

statue sculpture of a human or animal figure

Surrealist a group of twentieth-century artists who explored dreams in their art

texture in art, if you give something texture, you make it look how it might feel if you could touch it

Finding out more

More books to read

Heinemann Library's *How Artists Use* series:

- *Colour*
- *Line and Tone*
- *Pattern and Texture*
- *Perspective*
- *Shape*

Heinemann Library's *The Life and Work of* series:

- *Auguste Rodin*
- *Barbara Hepworth*
- *Buonarroti Michelangelo*
- *Claude Monet*
- *Edgar Degas*
- *Georges Seurat*
- *Henri Matisse*
- *Henry Moore*
- *Joseph Turner*
- *Leonardo Da Vinci*
- *Mary Cassatt*
- *Paul Cezanne*
- *Paul Gauguin*
- *Paul Klee*
- *Pieter Breugel*
- *Rembrandt van Rijn*
- *Vincent Van Gogh*
- *Wassily Kandinsky*

Websites to visit

www.eurogallery.org – this website lets you search the art collections of important museums and galleries across the whole of Europe.

www.nationalgallery.org.uk – this is the website of the National Gallery in London. All of the works in the collection can now be seen online.

Index

Titles in the *How Artists See* series include:

Hardback   0 431 93217 4

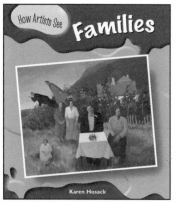

Hardback   0 431 93218 2

Hardback   0 431 93221 2

Hardback   0 431 93220 4

Hardback   0 431 93219 0

Hardback   0 431 93222 0

Find out about the other titles in this series on our website www.heinemann.co.uk/library